THE CALIFORNIA WORKERS' COMPENSATION SURVIVAL MANUAL

Powerful, time-tested techniques for surviving your California Workers' Compensation Claim

THE CALIFORNIA WORKERS' COMPENSATION SURVIVAL MANUAL

Powerful, time-tested techniques for surviving your California Workers' Compensation Claim

THOMAS K. LEDGERWOOD, ESQ.

CERTIFIED WORKERS' COMPENSATION SPECIALIST BY THE CALIFORNIA STATE BAR BOARD OF LEGAL SPECIALIZATION

WORD ASSOCIATION PUBLISHERS
www.wordassociation.com
1.800.827.7903

Printed in the United States of America.

ISBN: 978-1-59571-922-5

Designed and published by
Word Association Publishers
205 Fifth Avenue
Tarentum, Pennsylvania 15084

www.wordassociation.com

1.800.827.7903

TABLE OF CONTENTS

FOREWORD

"Knowledge is power."

- Sir Francis Bacon (English lawyer & philosopher, 1561-1626)

As they say, "Knowledge is power." Those who know the laws, facts, and procedures are the winners. Those who don't....well, you know what happens to them. There are specific techniques that can literally put thousands of extra dollars on the table and get your claim resolved much quicker, if you are paying attention to detail.

It has been the Wild West here in "compland" since 2004, when the "Govenator," Arnold Schwarzenegger, descended on working people across this state with his misguided idea of reform. As a consequence, theories on how to handle the devastation that has been wrought on your rights change daily, depending on the most recent decisions of the Workers' Compensation Appeals Board (WCAB), the California Appellate Courts, and the California Supreme Court.

It will take years to fix the mess - if we ever do. Most recently, Governor Brown has signed SB-863 into law, which will have wide-ranging consequences for all people injured on the job on or after 1/1/13. There are some good aspects to this new law, but the regulations interpreting it are being written as I write this second edition of this Survival Manual. As a result, the methods described in the following pages to deal with the current inequity could be out of date and obsolete tomorrow.

A very sober warning to all: it is a felony for anyone to knowingly file a false or fraudulent workers' compensation claim. The maximum fine for workers' compensation fraud is $150,000 or twice the amount of the fraud, whichever is greater (California Insurance Code Section 1871.4). Understand this: millions of dollars in grants are thrown at the local District Attorney's office to prosecute honest working people who get carried away. Don't fudge the facts. The last thing you want when you are hurt is having the locals coming down on you like a swarm of killer bees.

This manual is not a nuts and bolts book on how to handle your own workers' compensation claim. It is more of a map through the wilderness, showing you where to go and places to avoid like the plague. I also discuss alternate routes, if your benefits simply do not cut it. While I have done my level best to provide you with accurate explanations of the law, this manual is not a legal opinion on any issue or law and should not be relied upon as such. Finally, please note this manual contains a lot of upper-division techniques that are definitely not for rookies. Attempting them on your own would be like giving yourself a haircut or an appendectomy. Certain moves require the guidance of a seasoned expert. This manual is not a substitute for personalized advice from an officer with the WCAB or a knowledgeable lawyer. If in doubt, seek someone out.

Thomas Ledgerwood,

Attorney at Law,

Certified Workers' Compensation Specialist by the State Bar of California, Board of Legal Specialization

CHAPTER ONE

THE SECRET TO SURVIVING A CALIFORNIA WORKERS' COMPENSATION CLAIM

"If you don't know where you are going, you might wind up someplace else."

-Yogi Berra

The workers' compensation system has been around in California since the early part of the 19th century. Interestingly, the forerunner of all workers' compensation systems originated in Germany in 1884. California eventually enacted the Workers' Compensation Insurance and Safety Act of 1917.

To be brutally frank, the comp system is a down and dirty mechanism to prevent you from suing your employer for their negligence. In return, your employer provides some significant benefits to help you get back in the saddle. These benefits are nothing to scoff at; in some situations, they can go into the hundreds of thousands of dollars. No one gets rich; barely enough money is provided to help you squeeze by while you are recovering. Medical treatment is now provided on an almost Medi-Cal basis. If you approach the process intelligently, however, you can keep food on the table and a roof over your head during the process.

Unfortunately, the modern workers' compensation system has become a wilderness of red tape. You need a sober understanding of where you are going, the system's benefits (and where they fall short), how to quickly obtain those benefits, and where else to look for help.

You also need a plan.

The secret to surviving the workers' compensation system is to plot an efficient course through this land of law, procedure, and medical evidence. Failure to do so gets you stuck in "Comp Hell" (a place you definitely don't want to be). If you have never been this way before, you are at a distinct disadvantage. You need to educate yourself and pick a good path.

Your Objectives:

- Get the medical treatment you need to get back on your feet.
- Receive the maximum temporary disability (TD) benefit while you are recovering.
- Make sure you get the maximum dollar value for your permanent disability (PD).
- Take full advantage of benefits from other governmental programs.
- Settle your claim to provide for your future medical needs or cash out your claim by "Compromise and Release" (C&R) and be finished with the comp system.

Benefits mandated under the California workers' compensation system that can help you achieve your objectives:

Temporary Disability

If you are injured on the job and unable to work, you are entitled to temporary disability (TD). It will be paid at two-thirds of your normal salary subject to statutory maximums and minimums. TD is a non-taxable benefit. TD is now limited to two years, so people with more serious injuries are in deep trouble. More on how to deal with this problem in Chapter Two, "Keeping the Money Coming In."

TD will continue until you reach Maximum Medical Improvement (MMI), meaning that your medical condition or injury has reached a plateau, where no improvement is expected in the foreseeable future. Heads up: if you are unable to go back to work when you reach MMI, your TD will be unceremoniously shut down regardless of your ability to return to work. If you get lucky, the insurance company will send you a notice (with your last check). Thereafter, they are required to start paying you advances on your permanent disability (PDAs) every two weeks.

Medical Treatment

Under the California workers' compensation system, you are entitled to "all medical treatment necessary to cure or relieve the effects of your industrial injury" (LC Sections 4600-4603). This entitlement includes not only doctor bills but medicines, hospital costs, fees for lab tests, x-rays, MRIs, and other diagnostic procedures. You are also entitled to costs of mileage for going to and from medical appointments, the pharmacy, and med-legal evaluations.

However, being entitled to medical treatment under the system and getting it are two entirely different matters. The California legislature has given the insurance industry draconian powers to control their costs in this department such as:

- Medical Provider Networks (MPNs) (Think company doctor as your primary treating physician).

- Utilization Review (UR) ("No, you can't have this needed medical treatment as it is not 'evidenced based' and it costs too much").

- American College of Occupational and Environmental Medicine (ACOEM) Guides and the Medical Treatment Utilization Schedule (MTUS)--(Stingy, evidence-based treatment protocols that UR is based on--assembled by a pack of conservative pro-insurance physicians).

- Independent Medical Review (IMR), (Medical treatment disputes will be resolved by a doctor who will never see you).

Rest assured, you can get the medical treatment you need in a workers' compensation claim. You just have to know what you are doing. These benefits are all about saving money for big insurance companies. Now that SB-863 has been signed into law, huge changes will take place for folks injured on or after 1/1/13, but more on that in Chapter Sixteen, "What Did Arnold and Jerry Do to the Comp System?"

Permanent Disability

Permanent disability (PD) is compensation for your diminished future earning capacity. By the enactment of SB-899 in 2004, PD was slashed by between 40% and 70%, so a lot of attention needs to be focused on making sure this benefit is calculated fairly. Fortunately, there have been some really cool cases that have come down from the Workers' Compensation Appeals Board and Appellate Courts that put you in the position to fight back and get some meaningful numbers. Also, with the enactment of

SB-863, there will be promising scheduled bumps in this benefit for those injured on or after 1/1/13. This area is a minefield; please read Chapter Five, "Five Simple Ways to Maximize Your Permanent Disability," and Chapter Six, "Advanced Techniques for Increasing Your Permanent Disability Dollars."

Future Medical Treatment

If you settle your case on "stipulation," you keep your rights to future medical treatment open. The grant is for life. That used to mean something before SB-899 and the Schwarzeneggerization of the comp system. Drastic cuts were imposed on so-called "palliative" treatment such as physical therapy, chiropractic treatment, and acupuncture.

Sadly, keeping your medical treatment rights open sometimes only gives you the right to fight for future medical treatment, as it is now subject to UR, MPNs, ACOEM Guidelines, MTUS and IMR. There are ways to make it work for you. Don't get discouraged and give up. Read Chapter Three, "How to Get Effective Medical Treatment." If you have had it with medical treatment under the comp system, Chapter Fifteen, "Settling out Future Medical Treatment Rights," is required reading.

Supplemental Job Displacement Vouchers

Another cruel joke played on injured men and women in this state was the elimination of the Vocational Rehabilitation program in 2003. Back in "the good old days," injured workers that could not return to their old jobs had a simple retraining program to help them get back into the work force. Now we have Supplemental Job Displacement vouchers. For injuries prior to 1/1/13, vouchers range from $4,000 to $10,000, depending on an applicant's level of disability. Now it is a straight $6000 for all injuries.

It is not all bad. There still is hope. The trick with vouchers is combining them with other governmental programs to help you get back on your feet. See Chapter Nine, "Vocational Rehabilitation."

Helpful hint: It is all about quickly educating yourself. You will discover some very thoughtful directions on the specifics of a workers' compensation claim on the California Department of Industrial Relations website (dir.ca.gov), under the "Workers Compensation" tab.

CHAPTER TWO

KEEPING THE MONEY COMING IN

What you can do when temporary disability benefits stop and you have not fully recovered from your injury.

If you are unable to work at your job while you are recovering from an industrial injury, you are entitled to temporary disability (TD). The insurance industry had their way with the legislature in 2004 (SB-899), so now there is a two-year cap on this benefit. For injuries after January 1, 2008, TD can be paid out in broken periods for up to five years. There are a few very narrow exceptions to the two-year cap that simply don't apply to the vast majority of injured workers. You must make plans in the event that your condition prevents you from quickly reentering the work force. What happens if you are at the end of your two-year limit on TD, not finished with your medical treatment, and still unable to work?

A very important tip for your journey:

I heartily recommend that you file for State Disability Insurance (SDI) while you are on TD. Just do it! You can get an additional year of wage replacement if you qualify. It always amazes me how many people do not know about this benefit. Those deductions for "SDI" that have been withheld from your paycheck for all those years are finally going to pay off.

Normally you can't get TD and SDI at the same time (unless the rates are different). But, by filing for SDI as soon as possible (and informing them that you are currently receiving TD), you can lock in the date you applied.

The Employment Development Department (EDD) normally denies your claim if you are getting TD, but if you need to re-apply when your workers' compensation benefits terminate, your qualification will be determined by the date you applied for SDI. Eligibility for SDI is determined from previous work history. While you are on TD, you could fall out of your "insured status" period for SDI. In that case, you might be out of luck, as you would have no SDI benefits to fall back on. If you timely file for SDI, you can preserve your rights to collect SDI benefits when your TD shuts down.

The standard rule of thumb is that you must have paid into the SDI system for 17 months prior to your disability to draw the benefit. Take a look at your old pay stubs; do they note a deduction for SDI? If you paid this deduction for 17 months, you are golden! It is a huge tax-free infusion of cash that a lot of people simply do not think about. Get on your computer and go to the website for the California Employment Development Department (edd.ca.gov) to get the application process started. You can also find your "payment" history to see if you have paid into the program long enough to receive benefits.

Be careful here. You do not want to get paid TD and EDD benefits at the same time. If someone at the EDD is not

paying attention, this could happen. You cannot "double dip" (get TD and SDI benefits at the same rate at the same time). Someone who knowingly does so commits fraud. But you are entitled to the "differential" if your EDD weekly benefit is higher than your TD benefit.

The irony is that the insurance industry found a way to pawn off a legitimate expense of the workers' compensation system on the state and federal governments by setting up this two-year limit. As a consequence, it forces people to file for SDI and Social Security Disability (SSD) early. Injured workers have found themselves hung out to dry if they have a serious injury that will take longer than two years to recover from. With the new med-legal procedures and the powerful tools the insurance companies have been given to delay or deny medical treatment, it is it almost guaranteed that some cases will take a long time to settle.

If you are a state employee, you need to think about filing for PERS disability, the web site is calpers.ca.gov (STRS for teachers--calstrs.com). If you have a policy of short/long term disability provided as part of your benefits, you need to put applying for this benefit high on your "to do" list.

If it appears that your injury is serious enough to preclude you from doing any work, you need to consider an application for SSD/SSI. Application for these benefits requires claims within a specific time period and therefore requires prompt action on your part. I discuss the application process for SSD in Chapter Twelve, "How to Qualify for Social Security Disability."

CHAPTER THREE

HOW TO GET EFFECTIVE MEDICAL TREATMENT

Since the reforms in 2004 and 2012, California's workers' compensation system has become socialized medicine's evil twin. It is all about saving money for big insurance companies. Approval for basic medical treatment can drag on for months or years. Getting stuck in the muck of the system is now common, given the new med-legal procedures and the nasty tools the insurance industry has to restrict or deny treatment. So what happens to the person with a legitimate injury who fails to get appropriate treatment? Insurance companies now have Utilization Review (UR) and Independent Medical Review (IMR) to "deny, deny, deny."

Generally speaking, you have to treat within the Medical Provider Network (MPN). There are significant exceptions to this general rule. There are some fine doctors out there in the MPNs; others are not so good. Because they are paid directly by insurance companies, these doctors are not the advocates for their patients that they were in the past. I have witnessed notable exceptions, but sadly in the current system, if they overstep their boundaries they are labeled troublemakers and spit out of the MPN system like a bad seed.

Also, consider how MPN docs make their money. I have seen people languish for years without the appropriate referrals to specialists. Sometimes the doctor just is not doing his/her job in the face of significant neurological findings/studies that would indicate a referral to a specialist in the field of orthopedics or neurosurgery. All you can do is shake your head and get your client back on the path. That said, I have been told by thoughtful professionals that sometimes the best treatment is just time and the body's natural healing powers. Acute injuries may not justify expensive MRIs, as joints may be too "hot" to look at until swelling goes down. All I can say here is that you go to physicians for their training, experience and judgment; make sure you have a good one.

Dialing up medical treatment issues needs to be your first priority. Many come to us with simple denials such as: MRIs, EMGs, x-rays, epidural injections, or perhaps surgery. We like to get agreed medical evaluators (AMEs) on board quickly (if the carrier is willing). These folks are doctors that we have normally worked with for years. We allow them to do a medical evaluation and recommend a treatment plan. It can literally shave months to years off someone's claim.

The Most Powerful Tool to Get Timely Medical Treatment

Believe it or not, the most powerful tool in your kit to get adequate/timely medical treatment is the humble telephone. I have been in this field for two decades now, and I have discovered that the three most important elements to resolving a compensation claim are: people, people, and people.

Is something being denied at the pharmacy? You've got to get on the phone, take a very deep, restorative breath, and try to straighten out the issue with the adjuster. They have procedures that they must follow. They are people to;, respect that fact.

Many UR denials simply involve the UR doctor not being able to talk to your treating doctor. Or some other part of the puzzle is missing, such as a communication issue between the adjuster and the pharmacy. Getting on the horn is the simplest, most straightforward way of getting on track. Simply put, the vast majority of medical treatment issues are resolved by good old-fashioned communication.

SB-863

Everything changed yet again in 2013. Ever mindful of the bottom line, insurance companies pushed through SB-863. This law made for sweeping changes in the workers' compensation system. For disputes over medical treatment we now have "Independent Medical Review" (IMR). This system is a simple fraud on injured workers.

I am always suspicious about insurance industry moves, which usually involve cutting costs and benefits to injured workers. SB-863 takes away your right to get in front of a judge at the WCAB. In its place, there is now an HMO-style decision-making process for medical treatment disputes.

If you receive a utilization review (UR) denial, you have 30 days to appeal it in the IMR system. Thereafter, an "independent" doctor is required to make a determination based on a document review only. As of the writing of this book, approximately 80% of the UR denials were upheld by this star chamber of invisible doctors.

The determination of IMR is to be binding on all parties. Under Labor Code Section 4610.6(h), there are limited rights of review. There are huge due process issues with the appellate sections of this new law, and it is currently being challenged.

The Department of Industrial Relation's web site is a great place to start if you are planning to dispute a UR denial (http://www.dir.ca.gov/dwc/SB863/SB863_FAQs.htm).

Penalties

Sometimes you have to fight back. If you have an established medical treatment award, you can request that the insurance company be penalized for their unreasonable denial of medical treatment benefits. Penalties used to mean something before the reforms, as you could penalize the carrier for 10% of the "entire species of benefit" involving the denial or delay. If you had $100,000 in existing medical treatment, you could get a $10,000 award for a penalty on that amount, which really made folks on the defense side pay attention to detail.

Nowadays, an insurance company can only be zapped between 10% and 25% of the value of the denied benefit. If they are not paying for that $100 bottle of pain pills, you can only get between $10 and $25, so penalty dollars are not as motivational for insurance carriers as they used to be. On the other hand, suppose the value of the medical treatment was a $25,000 back surgery? We still have something to talk about here, just not in as many situations.

In summary, I can understand the staggering costs of medical treatment on workers' compensation claims and the need to make the system cost-effective for all. But the irony of the reforms was that it created an entirely new cost structure within the insurance industry for UR. Wouldn't it be more effective just to give people the medical treatment their doctors ask for and not make a case infinitely more costly by dragging it out? Unfortunately, sometimes you just have to push back until you get what you need.

CHAPTER FOUR

PANEL QUALIFIED MED-LEGAL EVALUATIONS

Question: What do you call someone who graduated in the bottom of his or her class in medical school?

Answer: "Doctor."

One of the more sinister aspects of the recent pro-employer workers' compensation reforms (SB-899) is how doctors are now chosen to do your med-legal evaluation. These evaluations are extremely important in a claim and can literally determine your fate in the comp system.

If you are unrepresented by an attorney, you can't get an agreement with the insurance carrier to have a respected doctor evaluate your medical condition. Such an arrangement is called an Agreed Medical Evaluation "AME." The nice thing about AMEs is that they are usually known quantities. They are doctors with whom both applicant and defense attorneys have worked with for years. These folks are typically fair and knowledgeable in their fields; they know how to apply the California Labor Code and case law in their evaluations.

The same cannot be said of Panel Qualified Medical Evaluators (PQMEs). In my experience, a frightening proportion of them simply don't know what they are doing. The insurance companies are not stupid. They see how conservative many of these panels are and many times will not even agree to an AME.

But it gets much worse. Orthopedic (bone) injuries account for about half the claims in California. A disproportionate percentage of the evaluations done on the orthopedic panels are performed by a small number of the most conservative physicians in the state.

Take for example the "Fresno doctors." To be called a "Fresno doctor" is not a compliment. Lawyers and judges love to joke about them. There are some notable exceptions to the "Fresno doctor syndrome," but they have become synonymous with the worst that is in store for people hurt on the job and badly in need of a thoughtful, reasonable med-legal evaluation.

For the most part, these folks do not care about the people they are evaluating. It is about making money by punching out as many med-legal evaluations as they can. These doctors will chop off unreasonable chunks of an injured worker's disability percentages based on apportionment. Many of their opinions are not "substantial medical evidence" as they are not supported by the "how and why" of their analysis. These doctors will earn a statutory fee for the evaluation and go on to the next case. Many do not know how the AMA Guides (the book for evaluation of impairment) work. Some will not use the proper instruments to evaluate impairment. They will frequently say "no" to industrial causation in cases that are clearly industrial. It is a vicious racket, and it is state sanctioned.

Here is a scary fact. If you pick an orthopedic panel and are sent a list from the Department of Industrial Relations (DIR) giving you a "choice" of three doctors to do your evaluation (your panel), you will not even know if you have chosen a Fresno doctor. This is because the doctors will use a local address on the panel forms! They really are not local doctors; they just get a day's worth of people to evaluate in your town and make it look like that is where their office is located.

There is a larger issue here with PQMEs. Some of these evaluators are okay; others are not. They have no inclination to give more accurate, higher impairment percentages in light of the Almaraz/Guzman opinions (discussed in Chapter Six, "Advanced Techniques for Increasing Your Permanent Disability"). As noted above, sometimes even attorneys have no choice and have to pick a panel. It can be a crap shoot if you don't properly vet these doctors and even then sometimes you need a little luck to boot.

> **Helpful hint:** Steer clear of the orthopedic panels, as they are infested with conservative doctors. A better choice for med-legal panels would be professionals in physical medicine, general medicine or chiropractics (even if those doctors are not perfect fit for your injury).

CHAPTER FIVE

FIVE SIMPLE WAYS TO MAXIMIZE YOUR PERMANENT DISABILITY

Rating 101: The Basics

This area can add or subtract a lot of dollars to or from your pocket. Permanent disability (PD) is payment for your reduced earning capacity due to your industrial injury. If you do not understand how "rating" works, you are at the mercy of the system. This section is required reading for the inexperienced.

Under the workers' compensation system, disability dollars for lost earning capacity are determined through a formula. The formula is set forth in the California Schedule for Rating Permanent Disabilities. The schedule gets modified from time to time. For this chapter, I will concentrate on the modifications that took place due to the changes in the law brought on by SB-899 in 2004 and most recently SB-863 in 2012.

If you are on your own, the insurance company should tender the QME report(s) to the Disability Evaluation Unit (DEU) for rating. The DEU is an independent body within the Department of Industrial Relations. They do not work for insurance companies. These folks read reports and grind out ratings all day. What they do is truly a specialty within a specialty. The trick is making sure they have all the medical information to do their job. This means that you have all compensable body parts in the mix and that the doctor evaluating you is applying current case law. Also, all appropriate AMA Guides findings need to be in the doctor's reports and everyone has your correct occupation and age.

Injuries Before 2013

For injuries on and after 1/1/05 and before 1/1/13, the formula combines several factors to come up with a disability percentage, which is then converted into dollars paid to you every two weeks. You need to carefully pay attention to all these factors – insurance adjusters do. As with most things in life, the devil is in the details. If you understand how the numbers flow together and how to maximize component parts, in many cases, you can increase the value of your permanent disability by the calculations alone. Here are the basic rating factors:

- Injured Body Part
- Impairment
- Future Earnings Capacity multiplier (FEC) (for pre-1/1/13 injuries)
- Occupation at time of injury
- Age at time of injury

Example

An example of a rating string for a lumbar spine (low back) injury for a 24-year-old recreational vehicle technician injured in 2006 looks something like this:

15.03.02.04 – 26 – [5] 33 – 370 G – 36 – 31 PD

Okay, it gets a bit technical, but you must understand this stuff. So let's take a hard look at this rating string:

15.03.02.04 is the injury code for a lumbar spine injury based on the range of motion method.

26 is the standard rating handed out by the AMA Guides for this injury.

[5] 33 describes the FEC modifier that boosts the standard rating of 26% to 33%.

370 is the occupational group number given for an RV technician, which increases the 33% to 36% due to the nature of the job.

31 PD is the final percentage for permanent disability given after the 36% was reduced for this fellow's age at the time of his injury. The value of his PD is $31,740.

So with this example in mind, let's dive into how all this works.

The Injury Code

The first question you have to ask yourself: is what part of your body is injured? Sounds simple, doesn't it? If you are not paying attention to detail, you lose. Given the fact that injuries are now evaluated through the AMA Guides "whole person" concept, you have to ask yourself if your base injury has affected other body systems. We call these "compensable consequences" and they can dramatically increase the value of your PD. In our example, the RV technician only had an injury to his back, but other systems could be involved that need to be separately set forth with their own injury code and combined.

One big mistake I see unrepresented workers make in this area is failure to identify all the component parts of their injuries. A compensable consequence is another body system that is affected by the underlying injury. It can make a massive difference in your rating.

I am going to be brief here, as this subject is covered in Chapter eight, "Recognizing Compensable Consequences." If you have a compensable consequence, you have an entirely separate rating string on this new condition/body part that can be combined with your underlying rating, which equates to increased disability dollars.

Most unrepresented workers get shot through the Qualified Medical Evaluation (QME) process like a cannon. Many times, the QME doctor pays absolutely no heed to peripheral body systems affected by the primary injury. The goal for many doctors is to crank out a report and get paid. Only the good ones really pay attention to this very important detail.

The AMA Guides are an impairment protocol that is decidedly pro-employer. This is how the standard rating is determined. By the way, I have had many cases where I got better results for clients under the new system, simply by tacking on every compensable consequence that was supported by the medical record.

The trap for the unwary or uninitiated is not carefully determining all body systems that the base industrial condition causes. Failure to identify them will cause the loss of big chunks of your disability dollars. No one is going to tell you about this unless a sympathetic rater from the Disability Evaluation Unit (DEU) or an Administrative Law Judge (ALJ) spots the issue.

Again, with our example of the RV technician who had a significant back injury and surgery, way too often the QME just evaluates the back, develops a report outlining it, and gets the statutory fee for the job. But what if other body systems have been affected by the back surgery in this example?

The question here is whether the back injury affected an independent neurological system. In the above example, a savvy evaluating neurosurgeon noted that the applicant had nerve root/ spinal sensory and motor deficits that significantly added value on a separate rating string. In this example, we tack on two elements that boost the value of the permanent disability by $6,440.00:

Lumbar – Range of Motion – Nerve Root/Spinal cord sensory

15.03.02.05 – 2 – [5]3 – 370G – 4 – 3 PD

Lumbar Range of Motion – Nerve Root/Spinal cord motor

15.03.02.06 – 2 – [5]3 – 370G – 4 – 3 PD

We combine all these impairments as follows:

31 C 3 C 3 = 35 Final PD

35% = $38,180.00

What about high blood pressure due to pain? How about internal organ problems developed through the use of the medications doctors prescribe? There is a substantial list of compensable consequences that must be separately rated. Don't put this manual down till you have completely reviewed Chapter Eight!

The Standard Rating

The standard rating is the percentage that a doctor describes as your impairment. It is the base percentage provided before modification by age and occupation. In our example above, it is the 26%. It is developed from the medical charts, physical examination, the doctor's application of the AMA Guides to Evaluation of Permanent Impairment 5th Ed. (AMA Guides), and current case/statutory law. Many times, you have to ask yourself if the doctor got this right. Did the doctor use the right tables in the AMA Guides? Is he or she familiar with the protocol? Many orthopedists might have missed the neurological compensable consequences the neurosurgeon described in the above example. A second set of trained eyes spotting something the doctor missed can be very helpful when submitting reports to the DEU (Disability Evaluation Unit).

Future Earning Capacity (FEC) Modifier

The insurance industry had to have a way to boost those stingy numbers that were laid out in the AMA Guides. They chose the FEC modifier based on the fabled and much maligned "Rand Study." It was another cruel joke on injured workers. While the FEC can boost underlying numbers up to 40% of baseline, the numbers are still woefully inadequate. The FEC in the above example is the bracketed 5 ([5]); it boosts the standard rating to give it a little more juice.

There are techniques to challenge the ultimate rating under the schedule, covered in Chapter Six, "Advanced Techniques for Increasing Permanent Disability."

The FEC modifier was abolished for injuries occurring after 1/1/13. But for injuries prior to 1/1/13, it is very much an issue. The analysis for a post 1/1/13 case doesn't stop there.

Determining Your Occupational Group Number

One of my very old rating manuals had a job description for a "Muleskinner" (someone who drives mules). How times have changed. The pace of change is so fast that the workers' compensation system can't keep up. Many jobs are just not listed in the schedule, which can be a serious problem for this modifier. In our example above, the RV repairman was a 370G.

This little item can make a huge difference in disability dollars and you need to pay close attention to it. The California Labor Code values impairments differently based on the nature of your occupation. A back injury to a laborer normally would be worth more than the same injury to an office worker. A brain injury to a doctor may be worth more than a similar injury to a hod carrier. It is just how the system works.

The $10,000 difference

Years ago, I had a client who worked for PG&E. He technically had the job description of "splicer" (someone who splices wires on the ground). But he climbed a lot of power poles. At the time of his injury, he was climbing a power pole. We argued the higher occupational variant of 482 for a "line installer-repairer," which added about $10,000 dollars in value to his claim.

If you are a baker, you are a 322, but if you are a "baker helper" (the guy who moves big bags of flour around), you are a 460. Let's say you are a secretary with a group number of 112, but the boss asked you to move a pile of furniture to a new office and you injure your back. Shouldn't you be a 560 "furniture mover"? Are you a truck driver (350)? What happens if you hurt yourself while you are lumping? (I think that is a truck driver helper, a 460!)

Get the idea? There are pages and pages of occupations described in the Schedule. There can be huge variances in the physical nature of the job descriptions involved, and failure to know the difference between them means you lose.

Age – the Older You Are, the Better

It may seem simplistic, but an incorrect date of birth can make a difference. The rating schedule rewards people who are 42 years and older by giving them an increase on their permanent disability. If you 36 or younger, you get correspondingly tagged for a reduction in PD. The age you were on your date of injury is the one that is used for this adjustment. Our RV technician got his numbers reduced substantially because he was 24 years old on the date of his injury.

This formula is based on the idea that as you get older, you have less time to adapt. At least, that is the thought behind the adjustment. Personally, I feel that younger people will have the impairments longer and should be compensated on that basis.

The 15% Bump

In the example of our RV technician, the 35% is valued at $38,180.00. PD can be increased by 15% if, within 60 days of reaching maximum medical improvement, this fellow's employer did not offer him regular work, modified work, or alternative work. But there is a catch; even if our technician has not been offered modified work, he does not get the "15% bump" unless his employer has 50 or more employees. This adjustment was eliminated when SB-863 went into effect in 2013. In this case, because our RV technician was not offered modified work, his base disability went from $38,180.00 to $43,611.29.

Injuries On and After 1/1/13 (SB-863)

The good news is that PD has increased overall by 30% for injuries on and after 1/1/13. The increase was phased in over two years, half in 2013 and the balance for injuries occurring in 2014. The current method for modifying the PD rate for lost earning capacity has been eliminated.

The bad news is that "compensable consequences" for sleep disorders and sexual dysfunction have been eliminated. Dollars for increased PD for psychiatric injuries will be limited to cases involving "catastrophic" physical injuries or a person who was a victim of, or a witness to, a violent crime.

The 15% bump-up/bump-down for PD has been eliminated for injuries on and after 1/1/13. In its place, there will be a $120 million dollar program designed to increase benefits for injured workers who suffer a "disproportionate loss of earnings" as a result of their injuries.

CHAPTER SIX

ADVANCED TECHNIQUES FOR INCREASING YOUR PERMANENT DISABILITY DOLLARS

This chapter strikes to the core of the David vs. Goliath struggle between the people the workers' compensation system was designed to protect and big insurance companies trying to save a buck.

The insurance companies won.

After the enactment of SB-899 in 2004, the value of permanent disability (PD) was slashed between 40% and 70%. Because of the way the numbers for PD are now described by the doctors, they can start out startlingly low. The system is now designed to take advantage of people who do not know any better. The question is, how do you increase those numbers to get them to more accurately reflect your disability?

Occult Knowledge…

No, I am not talking about devil worship here. Occult means a lot of things to a lot of people. Here, it means a secret only known by the initiated. The truth is that there are sound, time-tested ways to challenge the paltry results people are getting through the use of the AMA Guides. In this chapter, I will describe three of the most significant ways to challenge the silly numbers people are getting. These techniques are all upper division, "don't try this at home" methods for increasing PD. Consider enlisting the services of experienced counsel.

Understanding Recent Case Law Interpreting the AMA Guides

If you were injured on the job, you are entitled to compensation for your loss of earning capacity. How this was calculated under the pre-97 Schedule for Rating Permanent Disabilities (old schedule) was changed radically with the implementation of the American Medical Association's Guides to the Evaluation of Permanent Impairment, 5th Edition (the Guides), in 2004. As noted above, big chunks of PD dollars simply evaporated with this savvy insurance industry move.

The basic problem is that more often than not, a "straight" reading of the AMA Guides just doesn't cut it in terms of accurately describing work disability. The book, by its own admission, was not designed to do this:

> "The Guides is not intended to be used for direct estimates of work disability. Impairment percentages derived according to the Guides' criteria do not measure work disability. Therefore, it is inappropriate to use the Guides' criteria or ratings to make direct estimates of work disability."
>
> *AMA Guides to the Evaluation of Permanent Impairment, 5th Edition, p. 9*

Why is the state using the Guides to measure your disability? Well, because the Guides come up with some seriously stingy numbers for people with significant and limiting medical conditions. Employers simply do not have to pay out on claims the way they did before the reforms. The Guides have swept across the nation as the main way of describing permanent disability. California fell victim in 2004.

1) Almaraz/Guzman

As noted above, the Guides measure physical i*mpairment and its effect on activities of daily living* (ADLs), not work restrictions. The doctors determine the "whole person impairment" numbers by a physical examination. These numbers eventually get plugged into a formula to determine your disability, with sometimes seriously goofy results.

Almaraz/Guzman is a line of recent case decisions by the Workers' Compensation Appeals Board (WCAB) and the appellate courts. These cases allow a physician to come up with a more accurate result by looking at "functional loss" or comparing impairment by "analogy" to some other schedule or table in the Guides that is a more accurate description of your impairment. Essentially, an evaluating doctor can use clinical judgment (based on your ADLs) to depart from a straight reading of the Guides and provide more realistic numbers.

The *Almaraz/Guzman* formulation was codified in the legislature's most recent bill (SB-863), so the technique is here to stay. Evaluating activities of daily living (ADLs) is one of those little hidden techniques to give more rational results in the determination of your permanent disability. It is a useful tool to level the playing field if you are really hurt, and the numbers under the AMA Guides stink. The AMA Guides generally define ADLs as follows:

Self-care personal hygiene: Urinating, defecating, brushing teeth, combing hair, bathing, dressing oneself, eating.

Communication: Writing, typing, seeing, hearing, speaking.

Physical activity: Standing, sitting, reclining, walking, climbing stairs.

Sensory function: Hearing, seeing, tactile feeling, tasting, smelling.

Nonspecialized hand activities: Grasping, lifting, tactile discrimination.

Travel: Riding, driving, flying.

Sexual function: Orgasm, ejaculation, lubrication, erection.

Sleep: Restful, nocturnal sleep pattern.

2) Ogilvie III

When the legislature "reformed" the compensation system in 2004, they changed the basic way ratings were done to determine your disability. A "rating" is a formula that results in a string of numbers used to calculate permanent disability dollars. To get there, a "standard" rating is obtained from a treating physician or a med-legal evaluator utilizing the Guides to develop an impairment percentage. This impairment percentage is then modified by a Diminished Future Earnings Capacity (DFEC) multiplier, occupation, and age.

The DFEC is the insurance industry's answer to getting the impairment numbers from the Guides modestly increased based on the much maligned "Rand Study." The good news is FEC modifier was abolished for injuries occurring after 1/1/13 and replaced with better numbers due to SB-863. However, for injuries prior to 1/1/13, it is very much an issue.

The *Ogilvie* technique involves demonstrating an error in the rating string (see Chapter Five), the omission of medical complications aggravating disability not considered by the Rand Study, or a greater loss of earning capacity through the use of a vocational expert (VE).

This technique is not for all cases. It is an expensive and time-consuming route to take on only those cases that clearly warrant this approach. For starters, an individual must be precluded from returning to his or her old job due to an industrial injury. Furthermore, the basic rating(s) must not capture the essential lost earning capacity of an injured worker. If someone is going to take this route, he or she needs to be prepared to go to trial.

Under this technique, the VE is employed to take a hard look at an individual's injury and the numbers he or she got under a preliminary analysis under the AMA Guides. The VE compares the current earning capacity of an individual to that of "similarly situated workers."

If the VE determines that the industrial injury has caused a certain percentage of diminished future earning capacity that is greater than the scheduled rating, this percentage becomes the basis for an argument for a higher rating. The law is not well settled in this area.

3) Labor Code Section 4662

Finally, there is Labor Code Section 4662 dealing with "total disability," as set forth is this code section:

> "Any of the following permanent disabilities shall be conclusively presumed to be total in character:
>
> (a) Loss of both eyes or the sight thereof.
>
> (b) Loss of both hands or the use thereof.
>
> (c) An injury resulting in practically total paralysis.
>
> (d) An injury to the brain resulting in incurable mental incapacity or insanity.

In all other cases, permanent total disability shall be determined in accordance with the fact."

(a) - (d) are the obvious cases. What about the person who has had a failed back surgery, is on heavy narcotic medication, needs assistive devices to ambulate, and has qualified for Social Security Disability? You would think that person would be 100% disabled, wouldn't you? That is just not the way the Guides work. This person may be in the 80th to 90th percentile, but not 100%; a simply ridiculous result under the new impairment calculation protocols.

Under the WCAB's recent decision in *Boatright vs. Argonaut Construction,* the last sentence of 4662 has been given some serious new focus. In *Boatright,* the Workers' Compensation judge found an applicant to have a 92% level of disability. The WCAB concluded otherwise, finding 100% disability based on Labor

Code Section 4662 and the persuasive report and testimony of a vocational expert indicating that the applicant had a total loss of earning capacity.

CHAPTER SEVEN

UNDERSTANDING THE CONCEPT OF CUMULATIVE TRAUMA

It never ceases to amaze me how many people get led down the garden path by their employers. They are discouraged from filing claims on very basic, provable work injuries. I have seen countless situations where it was obvious the employee suffered "cumulative trauma" on the job and was told, "Gee, that is not work related. You need to file for State Disability and use your own insurance—good luck." It is employer fraud in my opinion. Some injures are easy to spot; we usually call them "specifics." A specific injury usually results from a specific event. Someone slips on black ice at work and suffers a shoulder injury. Or a lifting incident results in a spine injury.

The more difficult claims to spot involve a cumulative trauma period (CT), aka "repetitive stress injuries." It is a recognized legal theory of causation for workers' compensation cases right here in the state of California (Labor Code section 3208.1). For example, you have someone who does a lot of repetitive hand movements, such as a clerk in a grocery store, or a person on an assembly line. It can be as simple as a secretary or office person pounding out work on his or her computer day in and day out. Or an injury can occur by working at some crazy angle for hours on end. One day, the body rebels and the worker discovers a strange tingling in his or her hand, accompanied by significant numbness. The worker starts having problems holding objects and turning the doorknob when he or she gets home at night. This is classic carpal tunnel syndrome. The same thing can happen to your spine or the joints in your hips and your lower extremities. One day, a minor activity at work becomes the proverbial "straw that breaks the camel's back" and a significant workplace injury occurs.

Doctors say that the following conditions should raise a red flag:

> **Edema, tendonitis, carpal tunnel syndrome, cubital tunnel syndrome, thoracic outlet syndrome, DeQuervain's syndrome, stenosing tenosynovitis, intersection syndrome, golfer's elbow or medial epicondylitis, tennis elbow or lateral epicondylitis, reflex sympathetic dystrophy syndrome (RSD), radial tunnel syndrome and focal dystonia.**

Then there are the cases of occupational disease or exposure. A nurse works for years, snapping latex gloves on and off her hands thirty times a day. One day, the hands simply say no. They get red, chapped and sore. Infections develop and the hands refuse to be enclosed in latex again. It is called a "latex allergy" and it can be a severely debilitating condition.

What about a painter who works a power sprayer day in and day out, or someone who is exposed to dust and fumes? These work conditions can potentially cause significant respiratory problems over the years—or worse, cancer.

Filing a workers' compensation claim is a certifiable pain in the rear. I can understand someone's hesitancy to do so, but the consequences of not protecting yourself can be significant. Many employers, wary of yet another new comp claim, simply discourage their employees from reporting their conditions as industrial. As noted above, they encourage them to go on State Disability and use their private insurance. There is a problem with this approach. What happens if you lose your job and your medical insurance? No medical coverage in these days is a real problem, unless you can find some governmental program or a family member's coverage to treat under. Many governmental programs are income and asset dependent. If you have too many assets, or a spouse who is earning an income for the family, you could be out of luck.

The workers' compensation system operates as a social safety net. If you fail to timely claim benefits, you also lose out on valuable temporary disability rights (pay while you are recovering), permanent disability (payment for lost earning capacity), and perhaps a job displacement voucher (money to be used for retraining into a new field). Thousands and thousands of dollars of needed help can be lost through misinformation or ignorance. The trick is to understand the connection between work activities and injury. Don't snooze on your rights.

CHAPTER EIGHT

RECOGNIZING COMPENSABLE CONSEQUENCES

If you reviewed Chapter Five, you understand the basics of rating. Let's get down to the nitty gritty. Conservative forces in this state (think big business/big insurance) hammered us on this issue with the enactment of SB-899. This "reform" now requires the use of the American Medical Association's *Guides to the Evaluation of Permanent Impairment, 5th Ed. (Guides) to determine impairment/disability.*

It was a savvy political move and blue collar rip-off of statewide proportion. The imposition of the AMA Guides has resulted in simply ridiculous numbers. One of my clients, a very experienced ICU RN, had a serious knee injury resulting in a torn medial meniscus of her right knee. She was making $41.00 an hour and this injury was a career ender. She can't do her job as a nurse anymore given the physical restrictions of the condition. The Guides, under their diagnosis-based estimate, indicates that her injury is a 1% whole person impairment! One percent? That is the law now and it is nothing short of theft. To be sure, there are other theories out there to deal with this disparity (see Chapter Six), but this is the baseline here in California now.

Be forewarned: you must carefully pay attention to detail by identifying other body systems that are affected by an underlying industrial injury. We call them "compensable consequences." Much to our surprise, we have found that if we make sure all affected body parts are properly made part of a claim, we can sometimes get better results than we got under the old schedule work restrictions.

You need to understand how the Guides work. Under the Guides, you must look at the "whole person" when you are determining overall permanent disability. The trick is to ask yourself what body parts are affected by your underlying industrial injury and plead them (include them in an application for benefits). It can make a huge difference in overall disability and sometimes it is the only way to get decent numbers.

First, you need to take a hard look at the medications you are on. Suppose you suffered a painful back injury and have to take a variety of pain medications. Medications taken for pain can cause upper GI problems (GERD) or worse yet, lower GI problems (constipation/impaction/bleeding hemorrhoids). If the condition is serious enough, these are ratable disabilities and need to be worked up by a doctor and independently compensated.

For example, say someone has a claim for a very serious, painful neck injury; months down the line when she realizes that she is not returning to her old job, she becomes deeply depressed. Depression is independently compensable (and ironically, worth more than it was before the changes in the law), so it can be pled as part of a claim. I have seen cases, under the 2004 reforms (SB-899), where the psychiatric claim rates out higher than the post-surgical spine claim! It doesn't make any rational sense, but that is the way it can turn out.

The most current change in the law (SB-863) has changed much of what I have discussed here. As of 1/1/13, the compensable consequences of psyche, sleep disturbance, and sexual dysfunction are not independently ratable conditions. There is a small exception allowing only the most serious psyche injuries to remain independently ratable. Regardless, these conditions should be evaluated for medical treatment issues. In some situations, these conditions are directly caused by an injury and are not technically compensable consequences. In such a situation, they would be independently ratable.

This list of compensable consequences goes on to include, but is not limited to: high blood pressure, gait derangement, and headaches. It also includes dysfunction in the neurological, pulmonary, reproductive and internal organ systems (just to mention a few). Failure to have these conditions pled can result in a tremendous reduction in the value of the permanent disability.

As noted above, the real kicker in the change of the law post SB-899 is that the values for orthopedic claims (bone, tendon and ligament injuries) have been reduced drastically. The dollars awarded under a straight reading of the AMA Guides do not come near to adequately compensating people for their lost earning capacity. Careful attention needs to be paid to all reasonable compensable conditions in your claim.

CHAPTER NINE

VOCATIONAL REHABILITATION

"It's not whether you get knocked down; it's whether you get up."

--Vince Lombardi

When Life Gives You Lemons

What happens if your injury prevents you from going back to your old job? There is nothing like having the rug pulled out from underneath you in life. You spend years becoming good at something, and then suddenly you can't do it anymore. Industrial injuries can simply punch people out of the job market if they do not develop different skills ASAP.

A labor-disabling injury can be an opportunity if you look at it properly. When you can't make a living physically moving things around anymore, you need to learn new skills. What can you do if you find yourself here?

First, the Bad News:

Everyone wants to save a buck nowadays. Thanks to former Governor Gray Davis, the California Chamber of Commerce, and cigar-smoking, big business Republicans and Democrats across the state, the Vocational Rehabilitation program (VR) was phased out in 2009 (AB277 and SB288).

You are now left on your own to figure out how to get back to work. But, if you know what is out there, you will find some very clever ways to use a patchwork of state and federal programs to get back on your feet.

VR was a program that used to get people some quick training to get back in the work force. Some people abused it, but it was a huge benefit to motivated people who still wanted to work. Weekly money was provided while folks were training, via the "Vocational Rehabilitation Maintenance Allowance." There were vocational counselors and dollars to get training.

The good old days are over and the safety net is officially gone. If your employer doesn't have modified work, you literally have to hit the ground running as soon as you discover that you will be unable to return to your old job. If retraining is in order, then you really need to use the time you are getting temporary disability or State Disability benefits as a "scholarship" to retrain, if you can physically tolerate it.

The Good News:

To help folks who can't return to their old jobs, the workers' compensation system now offers the Supplemental Job Displacement Voucher (SJDV). My advice is to look at this spartan benefit as part of an overall strategy to help you get back to work.

The Voucher:

If you qualify for the program, the insurance company is supposed to send you the voucher. Another form to fill out, but well worth the time invested. You should receive the form 25 days after an award of permanent disability is made by the Workers' Compensation judge. For injuries prior to 1/1/13, the following chart shows your voucher amounts:

Disability Rating	**Voucher Amount**
Less than 15%	$4,000
16% - 25%	$6,000
26% - 49%	$8,000
50% - 99%	$10,000

For injuries prior to 1/1/13, you can't formally use a voucher until the end of your case, when there has been a formal finding regarding your permanent disability by a Workers' Compensation judge. People need to start thinking about the "next thing" the second it becomes clear that they will not be able to go back to their old job, but typically they have to wait for vouchers.

Under new Labor Code Section 4658.7, for injuries after 1/1/13, things get a lot better. You will be entitled to a flat $6,000 if your employer does not offer regular, modified, or alternate work within sixty days of the receipt of a permanent and stationary report from a doctor finding that your injury has caused permanent partial disability.

Also, expressly provided in this new code section is up to $1,000 for a computer and up to $500 as a "miscellaneous expense reimbursement or advance" payable upon request without need for documentation or an accounting. Such resources will help you to develop a résumé and start your job search.

Here is the catch—this benefit is not cash in the bank. It is a humble voucher requiring interaction with the workers' compensation adjuster. The voucher may be used for the following items:

1) Tuition for courses and/or skill enhancement. This is normally a school that is accredited or state-approved by the Bureau for Private Postsecondary and Vocational Education

2) Fees and taxes

3) Books and materials

4) Computer, if necessary for the program you have chosen

5) Vocational counseling services up to 10% of the voucher amount

6) Shipping fees for distance learning courses

7) For post-1/1/13 injuries, you can also use funds for purchase of tools required by a training or educational program in which you are enrolled.

There are many clever ways to use this benefit. How about an online vocational training course that requires a nice computer, for starters? As you can tell, the voucher is very restrictive in its use, so not a lot of people even take advantage of it. Statewide, only 10% of the vouchers are used by injured workers. You really need to think about linking this benefit with other programs.

Other Available Resources:

The California Department of Vocational Rehabilitation

You may qualify for additional assistance through the California Department of Vocational Rehabilitation (DVR). Google them; they have a nice web site. Go to "Resources" and get to work. No one said this was going to be easy – you are dealing with a state agency.

Board of Governors Waivers

If you are thinking about a more formal approach at your local junior college, you need to think about Board of Governors Waivers (BOG Waivers). Google Board of Governors Waivers or www.cccapply.org/money/fafsa.asp. This is a great little site, detailing requirements for the waiver. By qualifying for the waiver, you do not have to pay enrollment fees. But don't stop there! Consider financial aid on the federal level, such as Pell Grants, Perkins, and Stafford Loans.

Ticket Back to Work

If you are on Social Security Disability or Supplemental Security Insurance, you can consider the federal Ticket to Work program aimed at helping people get back to productive employment (www.dor.ca.gov/eps/ticket.htm).

Finding a New Path in Life

Understand that there is hope after a disabling injury. You just have to get off that couch and do something. You are the only person who can. You are not alone in this quest; you have people and resources at your disposal.

I will close this chapter with a story about my old client, Joe. Joe was in his early thirties pulling green chain at a local lumber mill, making "good money." Until the day he was zapped with 210 volts from an ungrounded piece of equipment. It seriously flayed his intercostals and almost killed him. No more green chain for Joe. We finished his case, set him up with an old style vocational rehabilitation plan and didn't see him for years.

The next time I saw Joe, he was strutting around in a charcoal gray three-piece suit. I stared at him in wonderment and asked, "Joe, what in the heck happened to you?" He explained to me that he had gotten some computer-assisted design (CAD) training and moved to Sacramento, where he had a fine job in an engineering company. He also had the foresight to start his own business on the side. He was clearly doing a fine job supporting his young family. That made me very happy. It is all about self-determination and pulling yourself up by your own bootstraps out there.

CHAPTER TEN

AVERAGE WEEKLY EARNINGS

The issue of "average weekly earnings" sounds really boring, but it is a wildly important subject that short changes people all the time. Spending ten minutes going over your pay stubs could make a huge difference in your overall benefits. You must pay attention to this detail.

I have the good fortune of knowing a lot of excellent, credible insurance adjusters. The vast majority of them are ethical folks just doing their job. Unfortunately, there are a few out there who are either unethical or just lazy. No one on the defense side is getting paid to maximize your benefits. Want to get cheated? Don't check the numbers.

Make no mistake of this fact: The income benefits you get paid on your workers' compensation claim (temporary disability [TD] and permanent disability [PD]) are directly linked to your average weekly earnings or "AWE." There are "maximum earners," "minimum earners" and a host of folks in between.

Minimum earners get minimum benefits under the system. Their PD is normally cut in half. Their TD is cut down drastically too. In-betweeners also lose dollars from every check they get from the carrier if their earning capacity is not fully accounted for. Maximum earners get the full TD and PD rates provided by the workers' compensation system, as long as they have their ducks in a row.

Make Sure All Earnings Are Calculated in Your AWE

Helpful hint: Sometimes an adjuster fails to find out that you have a second job. Earnings from a second job can have a huge effect on your AWE. The earnings from your second job should be added to the mix. I have had situations where the earnings from a second job doubled the numbers for clients.

Also, many other items are part and parcel of your earning capacity. Does your employer provide benefits? Let's say that you are managing an apartment house and the employer is providing you rent and utilities as part of your compensation. Tips are earnings, as are the value of meals provided by your employer. The value of these benefits needs to be factored into your AWE. What about all that overtime you earned earlier in the year? It should be counted, too.

Understanding How AWE Is Calculated

AWE is a trap for the unwary. Many adjusters (and defense attorneys) will try to push you into a slot that is not representative of your earning capacity. You need to understand how Labor Code Section 4453 works. Normally, AWE is calculated at the time of your injury, but not in all situations. The first question that needs to be asked is the nature of your employment. It is full time, part time, seasonal, or intermittent?

Full-time Workers

Full-time workers are easy. If you work at least thirty hours a week for five or more days a week, your AWE is determined by multiplying your actual daily earnings at the time of the injury by the number of working days in the week. Your weekly compensation will be two-thirds of that subject to the maximum and minimum rates set in the Labor Code. Just make sure that all your earnings are taken into consideration.

Don't be buffaloed if you have not worked for your employer for a full year! The issue is if *you were hired for full-time employment,* even if you were just recently employed. Insurance companies just love to call the employer and have them say your employment there was "temporary" or "seasonal" and hit you with lower rates based on your average earnings in the last 365 days before your date of injury.

Part-time Workers/Earnings at Irregular Rates

One way people routinely get short-changed is when the insurance carrier has incorrectly labeled them as part-time employees. If you are a part-time worker, your AWE will be based on your earning capacity at the time of your injury, looking back at the average of your total earnings for the past 365 days. There is a distinction between true seasonal employees and people who work intermittently, such as a job with a temporary agency. If you are a true seasonal employee, with no demonstrated long-term earnings history, you could get cut off your temporary disability during the off-season. Folks who are intermittent workers get an average and are not so exposed.

Not everyone earns at a regular rate. If you are paid on a piecework or commission basis, your AWE will be computed by taking the average of your actual weekly earnings for any convenient period that does not exceed one year.

In any event, getting put into the part-time, seasonal or irregular earner slot normally results in a markedly lower AWE number and a reduction in your overall benefits. Careful attention needs to be paid to the basic nature of your employment when you were hired. Also, take note of any changes in employment status from part to full-time employment during the time you worked for your employer.

When the Usual Formulas Do Not Work

The legislature threw us a bone on this issue, and it is a bright spot for all those people who have been laid low by bad times.

What if you are working a job that really is not paying you the money you normally could make when the economy is good? For example, you had to take a job making ten dollars per hour because times are tough and the economy is just not giving you the type of work you once did. In years past, based on your skills, you were earning thirty dollars per hour. It is all about earning capacity. Again, don't be fooled. Under Labor Code 4453(c)(4), your earning capacity is based on your actual earnings for all sources of employment. For example, you can go back to earlier years that are more representative of your earning capacity. Or, there could be consideration given to post injury earnings, or even potential future earnings if you were training for a new occupation that would be at a higher earnings rate or were slated for a raise.

CHAPTER ELEVEN

FINDING HIDDEN DOLLARS IN YOUR COMPENSATION CLAIM WITH THE SUBSEQUENT INJURIES BENEFITS TRUST FUND

Want the State of California to pay you a pension for the balance of your life? It happens all the time for those in the know.

Okay, you got zapped with "apportionment" in your workers' compensation claim (the doctor found you "100% disabled" but then went on to apportion 50% of your disability to non-industrial factors or an earlier injury). Not to worry, because you took the time to educate yourself by reading this manual. You understand that you can file a petition to join the Subsequent Injuries Benefits Trust Fund (SIBTF) to your underlying workers' compensation application.

Suppose you could find a way to get paid the difference between the apportioned 50% and 100%? It would be a massive bump in your case. How would that work? Well, the SIBTF is this wild little program that was set up under the workers' compensation system years ago allegedly to keep employers from discriminating against workers with pre-existing disabilities. Personally, I have not seen how that works in practice. However, it is a great rabbit to pull out of the hat when you get hammered by the ravaging effects of Labor Code sections 4663 and 4664 (which allows wholesale reduction in your permanent disability due to real or imaginary prior conditions).

The Recipe

-You had a permanent partial disability from any cause existing at the time of the "subsequent industrial injury" (the current industrial claim);

-The subsequent injury is work-related and resulted in additional permanent disability;

-The disability caused by the combination of both disabilities is greater than what would have resulted from the subsequent injury alone;

-The combined effect of the last (subsequent) injury and the previous disability or impairment is a permanent disability equal to 70 percent or greater; and

-The permanent disability resulting from the subsequent industrial injury has a "standard rating" (un-adjusted for age and occupation) of 35 percent or more, or five percent or more to the hand, arm, foot, leg, or eye if the prior disability or impairment affected the "opposite and corresponding member."

Sounds simple, doesn't it? Well, it is not. Like whipping up an outstanding omelet on a sunny Sunday morning, it takes a whole lot of time, chopping, dicing, and grinding all those ingredients together to get to the final product. We are dealing with a governmental agency of the State of California here—a certifiable bureaucracy. The pre-existing disability can be industrial or non-industrial and can arise from developmental, congenital, pathological, or traumatic causes. The seminal case for figuring this all out is *Franklin v. WCAB* (1978) 79 CA3rd 224.

Filing the appropriate pleadings to join the SIBTF is just the first step. Then they send you a letter with a page of documents that they want, along with a waiver so they can check into other state and federal benefits you are getting. You send them all this stuff and they seem to just sit on it. These folks are doling out limited public funds, so they are "tighter than the skin of a banana." They must dot all "i's" and cross all "t's" for a fully documented file.

The Rub

Ah, the devil is in the details. If you are on Social Security disability or PERS disability, you will be subject to an offset calculation that will reduce the money coming to you from the SIBTF while you are on these benefits. The credit they can claim is only applicable to the pre-existing disability. For example, suppose you are a deputy sheriff that files a workers' compensation claim. You have a pre-existing cardiovascular disability and later injure your back and knees resulting in a combined disability of 81%. While you are on Social Security disability or PERS/STRS disability, the SIBTF is entitled to a credit for the permanent disability that you received for the original (pre-existing) injury, but not for the disability based on the (subsequent) orthopedic disability. *Ybarra v. WCAB* (2002) 103 CA 4th. The SIBTF will claim a credit for the time you are on Social Security Disability or PERS/STRS disability. If you are on regular Social Security or PERS/STRS retirement, then the credit doesn't apply.

Be forewarned: The pace of getting this benefit is glacial. To get anything done, you need to gently push, push, and push. You get a lot more with honey than you get with vinegar, so be patient with these people. They are just doing their job.

Email weekly, call monthly, see what they need, and file for hearings often. It just takes a truck load of persistence. If you have a 100% case, you have to push it to trial and have a judge tell them what to do or nothing will ever happen.

By the way: the statute says permanent disability payments by the SIBTF may not be converted into a lump-sum payment (Labor Code Section 5100.5). Based on my experience, the SIBTF will disgorge lump sums. They are a state - mandated bureaucracy, but they are not foolish. Administratively, it might just be cheaper to cut one check. Or, sometimes there can be issues regarding their exposure, and discretion is definitely the better part of valor. A deal can be cut, putting a nice chunk of cash in your bank account.

CHAPTER TWELVE

HOW TO QUALIFY FOR SOCIAL SECURITY DISABILITY

"It ain't over till it's over."

-Yogi Berra

If you have suffered a total labor-disabling industrial injury, it is time to seriously think about your options. Keeping a roof over your head is the first priority, and that means intelligent planning early on. Benefits outside the workers' compensation system can take years to qualify for and have serious time limits involved for filing a claim. Snooze on your rights, and you will be out in the cold.

The trick is to file for Social Security disability (SSD) benefits along with your workers' compensation claim. If you do not need the benefit, you can always dismiss "Plan B" (your SSD claim) down the road.

If you are a public employee, you need to consider filing a PERS or STRS disability claim. The best piece of advice I can give here is never to quit your state job. You could lose valuable benefits if you quit before perfecting a claim for disability under the PERS or STRS systems. Large sums of money are at stake. Consider hiring an attorney who specializes in this area. Google "PERS disability lawyer" and start calling.

The benefit of doing a workers' compensation and SSD claim in tandem is that you can use the resources spent in the workers' compensation proceeding to develop the medical record on the SSD claim. This can involve thousands of dollars of medical work-up on the state level, paid for by the workers' compensation system.

In a workers' compensation claim, SSD is the eight hundred pound gorilla in the room that no one sees. People who have significant labor-disabling conditions must think about this benefit early. It can dwarf the benefits that they can get in a workers' compensation claim. In SSD land, a claimant will not only get monthly financial benefits until she reaches retirement age, she will also ultimately qualify for Medicare coverage.

You will qualify for Medicare two years after you have qualified for SSD. Purchase a decent Medicare supplement, and you are set. With Medicare, there is no coverage limitation to an injured body part as there is in state workers' compensation. While the Medicare system has its own challenges, it is not the "evil twin of socialized medicine" that the California workers' compensation system has become.

Like State Disability Insurance, SSD is driven by your work record. In an SSD claim, you need to have worked five of the last ten years to be insured under the system. If you have not, you could be out of luck. The only remaining benefit is Supplemental Security Income (SSI). That is why it is so important to file early while you are still insured! If you qualify for SSI, then you will automatically qualify for MediCal. SSI is an income-based benefit. It is federal welfare. Generally, if a spouse or a member of the household is making a significant income or you have more assets than allowed by the program, you don't qualify.

The Secret Sauce

Understanding the sequential evaluation process is like discovering the colonel's secret blend of "11 herbs and spices" or figuring out how they make an Orange Julius taste so good. Working with the legal elements for SSD qualification is a lot like doing a great job following your favorite recipe. The sequential evaluation process is the Social Security Administration's (SSA) recipe for denying or qualifying someone for SSD.

Another sneaky ingredient in the mix of obtaining benefits is the unspoken rules within the SSA. One of my clients was on the "inside" of the SSA doing claims work. This insider advised me that her manager would constantly ask about her "numbers" (that is SSA code for claim denials). You need to be equally tenacious on your end.

When you apply for SSD, there are four levels of appeal to either grant or deny your benefits. If your claim is denied, you can request reconsideration. If your claim is denied again, you can get a hearing before an administrative law judge (ALJ). If you are not happy with the ALJ's decision, you move up to the Appeals Counsel, then, the 9th Circuit Federal Court of Appeals. You will find it an obscure process cloaked in vague denials. The trick is to keep appealing and never give up!

I can state categorically that to be qualified for the benefit, you normally need to have your medical condition well documented and have the appropriate facts on your side. If you are under 49.5 years of age you will have to demonstrate that your residual functional capacity is that of a sedentary occupational base that is significantly eroded. This would be someone that can only sit or stand comfortably for fifteen minutes. Or, you can demonstrate a "listing level disability."

If you are 49.5 years or older, things get a lot easier as your residual functional capacity (RFC) can be greater and you can still qualify. Who said getting older is all bad?

The Sequential Evaluation Process:

Step 1 The first decision concerns determining if you are involved in "substantial gainful activity" (earned income). Check the SSA website for current limits; for 2014 it is $1,070. If your earnings are not above this amount then you get to go to step 2.

Step 2 Do you have a severe impairment? Normally this is a condition that will keep you from working for a year or more or result in death. If the answer is yes, you get to go to step 3.

Step 3 Does your medical condition meet or equal an impairment described in SSA's "Listings of Impairments"? If so, you can stop here--you win! If not, go to step 4.

Step 4 Can you perform the easiest job you did in the last fifteen years (past relevant work)? If so, you just got denied. If not, go to step 5

Step 5 Can you do other work existing in the national economy considering your residual functional capacity (RFC), age, education, and work experience? If you can, you will get disqualified. If you fit into one of the slots on the

"Grids," (a decision making model based on your RFC, age, education and transferable skills) you are approved!

Sounds easy, doesn't it? Sometimes it is. Some people luck out and get some reasonable evaluator in the SSA and they are magically qualified. This is a game changer for those folks who were facing the prospect of living under a bridge. In other cases, it is like pulling teeth and you get to push issues through all of the levels of appeal.

I see a lot of clients these days completely short-changed by the workers' compensation system. Oftentimes, permanent disability under the AMA Guides impairment rating protocol doesn't accurately capture the nature and quality of someone's condition. Even with the addition of SSD benefits, there might not be enough money coming in to keep a roof over one's head. People in this situation should consider work that keeps them under the "substantial gainful activity" radar. We recommend that our clients take a trip down to Barnes & Noble, go into the self employment section, and start thinking about a home-based business. This constitutes work that they can do when they feel up to it, on their own terms.

The good news is that if you have the facts on your side, you can win one of these claims. However, it is very upper division stuff and this is not an area to "go it alone." If you are denied benefits on the initial evaluation, then you seriously need to consider getting competent counsel to help you

CHAPTER THIRTEEN

SURVIVING YOUR DEPOSITION

So there he was, not exactly a championship bull rider, but putting on a good show--riding a large, angry, snorting bull in front of a few thousand people at the Red Bluff Round-Up.

The problem was he had recently made a workers' compensation claim for an alleged "serious" back injury. We used to call this "felony stupid" in the years I spent in the District Attorney's office. Law enforcement types came down on this fellow hard. Use the Google search terms "Video Tape Workers' Compensation Fraud" and watch the You Tube clips. How can people be so foolish?

If you are not represented and your deposition gets set, you really need to consider getting competent counsel. One of the most dangerous times in a workers' compensation claim is at deposition. Most people have never been deposed. They do not know how the process works and what the rules are. More importantly, they do not have the judgment that you get when you have sat through a couple thousand depositions.

A deposition is a formal legal proceeding. Pointed questions will be asked of you. You must answer these questions under oath with a court reporter present. As a matter of fact, a deposition is just like being in court, minus the judge and jury. There are simple, honest techniques that can be employed to protect the deponent (you) from being set up.

First, let's talk about the law. It is a crime to misrepresent an industrial injury for financial gain. As a matter of fact, it is a felony for anyone to knowingly file a false or fraudulent workers' compensation claim. The maximum fine for workers' compensation fraud is $150,000 or twice the amount of the fraud, whichever is greater, and up to three years in jail. While not an exhaustive list of California code sections carrying criminal sanctions for fraud (there are a bunch of them out there), here are the main ones: Insurance Code Sections 1871.4 and 1871.5, California Labor Code Sections 3820-3823, California Penal Code Sections 550 and 549.

Insurance Commissioner David Jones, in a news release dated July 5, 2011, announced a 32 million dollar grant to "district attorneys across the state" to prosecute workers' compensation insurance fraud. The allocations to Butte, Shasta and Tehama Counties alone were $463,950. This is not something to take lightly. I have had clients do jail time and suffer some significant fines for misrepresenting their claims.

Credibility

The most important quality a person brings to a workers' compensation claim is credibility. You can prove things in a workers' compensation claim that are not susceptible to absolute scientific verification if a physician and a judge believe that your complaints are valid. If people are not truthful about their condition, they lose that all-important quality and run the risk of criminal sanctions.

Sub Rosa is the Latin for "under the rose," or "secret." Many of my defense colleagues confirm that in about 15% to 30% of workers' compensation claims, the carrier will run *sub rosa* video on an applicant. They record out of vans, cheap foreign cars, or briefcases, "60 Minutes" style.

If you are outdoors in a place where you do not have a "reasonable expectation of privacy," it is open season on you. That is the general rule. To be sure, there are limits to what an insurance company can videotape. They cannot videotape into your home. That would be an invasion of privacy and subject the investigator to criminal or civil sanction.

I have had clients videotaped going into their doctor's office (a prime time for video). I have had clients videotaped coming into my office (just before their deposition). Most video I have viewed is shot in front of their own homes. A defense attorney does not even have to inform me prior to the deposition that video has been run on a client.

I advise many clients who have cases that are approaching the 70% to 100% permanent disability mark that it is not a question of if, but *when* an investigator will shoot video on them. There is simply too much money on the line for the carrier not to test credibility. If a claim is denied or if an employer or insurance company doesn't like the injured employee, it is most likely going to happen.

The truth is most video recordings simply don't matter. So they have you on tape, going to the local store, pumping gas, getting into your car, shooting the bull with the neighbor. When shown this stuff, doctors yawn and normally say that it doesn't change their underlying opinions. Many situations can be explained by the effects of pain medication. Most of this stuff can be explained by the facts. I had a client caught toting around what looked like a heavy ice box. Well guess what? It was empty when he plucked it out of the back of his car and only weighed about eight pounds. Nice try.

But what if the video shows someone doing sustained work activities that are markedly more strenuous than the limitations they reported to a doctor? Or what if they have reported to an insurance company representative or testified in deposition to limitations that are clearly disputed by a video? That is a completely different story altogether.

One unfortunate fellow here in the North state reported in his deposition that "he always used his cane." Period. Sure enough, in comes the video showing him packing a cooler he-man style into his boat. He was clearly not using a cane. He was popped for a felony. Fortunately, the judge did not impose jail time, as the fellow had a legitimate, documented back injury. The problem was he got caught (intentionally or negligently) misrepresenting the nature of his limitations and now he has a felony record.

After SB-899 (see Chapter Sixteen), the deposition has turned into a giant fishing expedition for the defense. They are trying to find out everything about you that they can to reduce the value of your claim. They are particularly interested in preexisting conditions you may have suffered to the same body part or preexisting settlements so they can reduce your permanent disability through apportionment.

Though the deposition appears informal, it is no less important than a hearing before a judge. The deposition "freezes" your testimony. After the deposition, a transcript is prepared and given back to you for corrections. You have thirty days to make the corrections to your deposition. Sometimes you need to change your testimony, as it was not accurate or there was an error on the record. No worries. But, should you make a correction of a material nature, you need to know that the defense attorney could comment upon that correction at a subsequent hearing (to impeach your credibility). So it is very important to give your best testimony at the time of the deposition.

Ledgerwood's Seven Golden Rules to Shark-Proof Deposition Testimony

1) Avoid absolutes in your responses

To questions regarding past medical condition(s) or workers' compensation claims, "never say never."

It is common for people to innocently forget or misrecollect past things and events. The trick is not to let a defense attorney turn innocent misrecollection into an item used to discredit you or worse yet, serve as the basis of a criminal prosecution.

For example, what happens if you are questioned about a pre-existing industrial injury or physical condition that you have genuinely forgotten about? How do your protect yourself from the unknown? Let's say you had a minor workers' compensation claim twenty years ago to the same body part you are currently claiming. You have completely, innocently forgotten about it - period. The defense attorney asks the question: "Have you ever filed for a workers' compensation claim in the past?" What should be your answer?

#1) "No."

Or,

#2) "I do not recall"

Remember, this is a question regarding facts so old that you genuinely and innocently forgot about it. Which answer protects you the most? Answer #1) "No" is absolute and is a bit more difficult to explain. Eventually, everyone finds out that you did in fact have a preexisting workers' compensation claim and it looks like you were lying or perjuring yourself. Answer #2 gives you a little better pillow to fall on down the road if you need to explain your response.

I am not talking about being sneaky or dishonest here. I am talking about having a thorough understanding of the consequences of answers to a deposition and preparing yourself for the fact that you are human and your memory is not perfect.

Defense attorneys love to ask questions about past medical problems. They get paid to dig deeply into medical history and see if they can demonstrate previous physical limitations regarding the subject injured body part. If you can't remember, you can't remember. Don't let the defense attorney put words in your mouth.

To questions regarding physical limitations, avoid absolutes such as "always," "I cannot," or "never."

This is what keeps me up at night. If there is an area in a deposition a client is going to get in trouble on, it is squaring the physical limitations he or she describes against the potential of a video contradicting his or her testimony.

The basic problem is that you are describing a body part that really hurts and you are asked what you can or cannot do. You say "no" you can't do the activity because it hurts. It is an innocent overstatement because in reality you could do it if someone's life depended upon it. For example, you hurt like the dickens and you avoid lifting like the plague, but what would happen if your house was burning down and you had to haul a family member out? If you could physically do it, you would, wouldn't you?

Recall the fellow above. His testimony was "I always use a cane." He was guilty of answering in the absolute—"always." Whether it was innocent or not, it was a fool's answer. Life is rarely played out in absolutes; protect yourself. The man had a serious documented back injury; a very simple fix would have been the following answer:

> "Some days I need my cane because of pain; some days I do not. It depends on how I feel."

Problem solved. The little trip he took to load the cooler into his boat would have been a lot more explainable. Defense attorneys love to take depositions. Blah, blah, blah for hours! Don't they ever read their files? Most of what they ask is documented in the materials they already have. But on they go, droning on for half a day. Remember, they get paid by the hour. Then, like a stealth attack, they ask some very pointed questions about what you can or can't do. The red flags go up on my end of the table. "Incoming!" This is where you need to be very, very careful about your answer(s).

"Can you lift a forty-pound bag of dog food?" "Do you mow your lawn?" "Can you wash your car?" "Do you garden?" "Can you lift a child?" These are "credibility questions" and if the answer is a simple "no" to any of these questions, and there is videotape to the contrary, your case is compromised.

Again, it is a question of avoiding absolutes. "Can you lift a bag of dog food?" Even if it would physically hurt you, but you're physically capable of doing the act, the answer is definitely not "no." Why would it be? You can lift a forty-pound bag of dog food (and they might even have you on tape doing it). The physical act might be very painful, but again—if your house were burning down, you would find a way to scoop up that kid and bring her to safety, pain or no pain.

Assuming you are capable of the act, a better answer would be, "yes, but it would be very painful," or "it depends on the amount of pain medications I am using," or "I have good days and I have bad days, on a good day I could lift a bag of dog food, but I will probably pay for it later."

Qualify, qualify, and qualify. Depositions are sterile, artificial, non-real time traps for the unwary and inexperienced. Make sure your answers are an accurate reflection of your physical reality and not a knee jerk response to an off the cuff question.

2) Do not volunteer information

Defense attorneys are paid by the hour. If you volunteer information, they will continue deposing you until they run out of questions. Do not provide them with any information not asked for. Keep your answers brief. Do not explain yourself unless you are called upon to do so.

For example, if the question is, "What color is the sky?" your answer should be, "blue." Period. You are not to go on to explain current weather conditions and the five-day forecast. Let them drag the information out of you. Be appropriately guarded. Keep your answers short and to the point.

3) Do not guess

It is natural for people to guess in day-to-day conversations. Unfortunately, guessing at your deposition can cause problems. As indicated above, a deposition is a statement that is taken under oath and under the penalty of perjury. The deponent must have a basis upon which to give testimony. You must have listened to, smelled, felt, tasted, or experienced what you are testifying to in order to have a "foundation" to make a statement. If you don't have a "foundation" to testify from, you are guessing.

People are frequently asked to give testimony on times, speeds, and distances. If they have the foundation upon which to testify, it is okay to answer the question. A defense attorney is entitled to your best estimate if you can give it. If you are estimating, be careful to give yourself some wiggle-room when you are answering. "Approximately," or "about," or "to the best of my recollection," are good ways to qualify your answer in areas where you cannot be exact.

It is okay to tell the defense attorney, "I don't know."

Here is something really sneaky that defense attorneys love to do, which completely drives me up a wall: They start asking you about your medical history say ten years ago and expect you to have "total recall" as to a doctor's visit or an event. Problem is, you have absolutely no idea what you told your Doctor ten years ago, but feel like you should answer so you do not look stupid. You get this quizzical look on your face and the defense attorney pulls out a copiously tagged medical record from his/her briefcase and asks you "You told Dr. So & So on such and such date that you can't do this or that, didn't you?"

Well, it was ten, twenty, or thirty years ago and you do not in fact have the slightest idea of what you told old So & So. Do you agree with the defense attorney when he says, "Does that sound about right?" No. You advise him/her that you do not have a "present recollection" of the conversation/event. Do not let the defense attorney put words into your mouth. He or she is trying to establish preexisting limitations or conditions to reduce the value of your case.

4) Be scrupulously truthful about your medical history

Defense attorneys earn their living by scouring the countryside for your medical records. If you had a pre-existing accident, injury, or settlement, they will find out about it. They have broad subpoena power, which allows them to track down most medical and legal information on an individual.

This is another area where clients can hurt their cases—failure to be forthcoming about their medical history. Again, the most important thing that you bring into your workers' compensation claim is your credibility. If you fail to disclose pre-existing medical conditions that you know of, you can destroy or compromise that all-important quality.

5) Make sure you understand the question

Sometimes people will answer a question even when they don't understand it. A judge will assume that you understood the question if you answered it. Do not be afraid to ask the defense attorney to clarify his or her question.

6) Assume your life has been on videotape

As noted above, insurance companies routinely conduct surveillance footage on injured workers. Make sure your testimony regarding what you can and can't do is consistent with what you do outside your own home, in front of windows, around town, etc. It is unlawful to shoot video in a place that you have a "reasonable expectation of privacy." If this happens, you should consider a suit against the insurer and investigator (California Penal Code section 632 and Civil Code section 1708).

7) Understand that the defense attorney is not your friend

Some defense attorneys are very friendly and gregarious. Some are not. Regardless, I always have my hands on my wallet when I am around these guys. Personally, I worry most about the friendly ones, as they make clients relax and talk more. Defense attorneys are paid to find anything and everything that can be used to reduce the value of your claim. You need to be very careful when answering their questions or relating to them in the same room.

Other good ideas:

It is really hard to mess up your deposition, if you are doing your best to honestly answer the questions that are asked. Just do your best and get a good night's sleep the night before. Depositions usually are over within two hours.

Most times, clients are on medications. It is OK to have medications on board during your deposition so long as you can understand the questions and give thoughtful answers.

A deposition is not an endurance test. You should break at least every hour, more frequently if you are uncomfortable. Feel free to stand up or change positions during your deposition.

Remember to submit a mileage claim for your travel to and from your deposition. You are also entitled to reimbursement for lost wages incurred during attendance at your deposition.

Dress conservatively and neatly, as you would for a job interview. You should convey an image of a serious, careful individual, not one who is indifferent.

Be prepared to discuss the nature of your injuries and be able to describe the pain and discomfort you experience. It is advisable (to the extent that you can) to be prepared to state the medical doctors you have seen and the nature of the treatment you received. It is OK if you can't recall all dates and times. Just be as prepared as you can to address your general treatment course.

If you are handed a document during the deposition, read it carefully before answering questions about it.

Avoid inappropriate language such as obscenities and racial slurs in answering questions. Remember, you are "on the record."

Losing a million dollars in two hours

Just a final note: One of my cases had a lump sum permanent disability worth well over a million dollars. That was before the two hour deposition and the video that was delivered to my office a few weeks later. The video showed my client doing work that was completely inconsistent with deposition testimony. The claim settled for a fraction of what it was worth.

My advice to clients is to be scrupulously honest about the physical limitations they describe. Be wary of what they do outdoors during the pendency of their claim. Be very circumspect in describing their limitations in deposition. It pays to be up front and accurate. Let the doctors decide and the lawyers fight about it.

CHAPTER FOURTEEN
WHEN GOOD EMPLOYERS GO BAD

"Life is tough, but it's tougher when you're stupid."

-John Wayne

Extraordinary Remedies Inside/Outside the Workers' Compensation System

Sometimes employers do foolish things. Generally speaking, the workers' compensation statutes prevent people from suing their employers. The benefits an injured employee gets in a workers' compensation claim are said to be their "exclusive remedy." However, there are limits to the immunities employers enjoy under the system. You should know that there are "extraordinary remedies" available to you within the workers' compensation system. There are also civil remedies that fall outside the system that can dwarf the benefits obtainable though a humble compensation claim. Any time you have a foolish employer, both remedies must be investigated.

Serious and Willful Misconduct

The first question to ask is how your on-the-job injury occurred? 99.9% of compensation claims are the type that involves an "accident" where no one is to blame. Some accidents involve employer "negligence" or even "gross negligence." These claims are normally handled by regular procedures because the workers' compensation system is supposedly no-fault.

But what if your employer has "consciously disregarded your safety interests" and you were injured? We are talking criminal stupidity here (or something very close to it). There are some situations where an employer knowingly puts an employee in a dangerous situation. If the employer does, and the employee is hurt, the employer could be liable for Serious and Willful Misconduct (S&W). If you are injured in this fashion, you could be entitled to an additional check equivalent to half the entire benefits that were paid on your claim. That includes the costs of medical treatment, job displacement voucher, temporary and permanent disability. In some instances, it can be a very big check indeed.

Example

I had a client who was directed by his supervisor to get into a huge excavator bucket and work out of it on the side of a mountain (not an OSHA approved man-basket). My client was "low man on the totem pole" and was directed to do this. When they were finished with the job, the supervisor/operator decided to take the employee "for a ride" by twirling around the excavator while he was in the bucket. At the end of "the ride" he dumped my client out on the ground from some height. The problem was, he was tethered into the bucket with a strap and suffered a significant back injury when the tether played out like a yo-yo. We got him an additional $100,000 over and above his compensation claim.

An S&W is a benefit that is not insurable. In other words, the money comes directly out of the employers' pockets. Naturally, the employer is going to fight all issues. There are three ways of demonstrating employer liability. The first is demonstrating that the employer's conduct was "willful" in that the employer actually knew of the dangerous condition and deliberately failed to take action. Another approach is to demonstrate that the employer failed to act even though it had information or knowledge that serious injury would probably result. Finally, liability can be found if it can be demonstrated that an employer was or could be charged with a "serious" violation of a Cal/OSHA safety regulation.

There is a one-year statute of limitations to file an S&W. In most instances, you have one year from the date of the wrongful conduct to file and serve a petition with the Workers' Compensation Appeals Board (WCAB). Failure to do so normally means you are barred from maintaining such a claim and out of luck.

If you are hurt by the conduct of a co-employee, you might be out of luck unless you can demonstrate that this person had managerial responsibilities. In order to prevail it must be demonstrated that the employer's conduct was committed by the owner, a named partner (in a partnership), or, in the case of a corporation, a person who was a "managing representative" (think foreman with hiring and firing responsibility, supervisor or higher) of the employer.

Labor Code Section 132(a)

Occasionally, people get fired in association with the filing of a workers' compensation claim. This is a huge red flag. Any time this happens, you must take a hard look at the facts and ask what really occurred. Were you fired in conjunction with the filing of a workers' compensation claim? Or, after filing a workers' compensation claim, were you treated differently from other employees due to such a filing? There could be the possibility of a Labor Code Section 132(a) claim for discrimination.

If you prevail on such a claim, you could be entitled to reinstatement of your employment, back pay, and up to $10,000 in penalties against the employer.

One way to prove such a claim is to demonstrate that the employer fired or demoted you due to the fact that you filed a workers' compensation claim. This is not so easy, as you have to get lucky and have some insider "tell it like it is" (testify that the employer verbalized a motivation to fire or demote).

There is a more subtle way to prove a violation of this statute by employer conduct aimed at treating individuals who file workers' compensation claims differently than other employees. Employers might cut their pay, demote them, or subject them to unreasonable changes at work like changing shifts without reason.

It is all very sneaky on the part of the employer. It is very hard to prove these claims and there can be legitimate business reasons for layoffs or disciplinary actions against employees that can operate as a complete defense.

However, if you have a clean work record, your employee file is chock full of commendations, you have a substantial work history with the employer and the discriminatory conduct is close to the time of your comp claim, you need to seriously consider doing something about it. Like an S&W, under normal circumstances you must file such a claim with the WCAB within one year of the discriminatory conduct or you lose this right.

ADA and FEHA claims

There are laws outside the workers' compensation system that protect you from being discriminated against by your employer for a disability. The protections from such conduct are on both the federal and state levels.

Americans with Disabilities Act

The Americans with Disabilities Act (ADA) is a federal program that George H. W. Bush signed into law in the early 90s. To charge an employer with an act of discrimination on the basis of disability, a claim must be filed with the Equal Employment Opportunity Commission (EEOC) within 180 days of the discriminatory conduct.

To utilize the ADA, the employer must have fifteen or more employees and must have discriminated against an employee in any aspect of employment such as hiring, testing, application, evaluation, training, layoff/recall, compensation, leave, and/or benefits.

An employee who prevails on an ADA claim could be entitled to compensatory and punitive damages between $50,000 and $300,000, reinstatement, back pay, payment for loss of future earnings, legal fees, expert witness costs, fees, and court costs.

The California Fair Employment and Housing Act

Similar rights are available to employees suffering from discrimination on the state level through the Fair Employment and Housing Act (FEHA). FEHA has remedies that are similar to the ADA. If an employer fails to make a "reasonable accommodation" for an employee with a disability, they could be in violation of the Act. To make a claim, generally speaking, you must file with the California Department of Fair Employment and Housing (DFEH) within one year of the discriminatory act.* Thereafter, you receive a right-to-sue letter and have an additional year to file a complaint in civil court.

*There are exceptions for the "continuing violation doctrine" and "equitable tolling."

CHAPTER FIFTEEN

SETTLING OUT FUTURE MEDICAL TREATMENT RIGHTS

True luck consists not in holding the best of the cards at the table; luckiest is he who knows just when to rise and go home.

-John Ray, English naturalist (1627-1705)

When to "Hold 'Em" and When to "Fold 'Em"

Many people, fed up with the way the California workers' compensation system now doles out medical treatment, are choosing to cash out. They would rather self-direct their medical treatment by having a fund of money for this purpose instead of having an insurance company calling the shots on medical treatment. Other people simply need to put food on the table and have no other choice. Either way, it is a gamble to walk away from the deep pocket of an insurance company when you need continued medical treatment.

Regardless of a person's motivation, giving up medical treatment rights is a huge decision, as it means no more treatment coverage from the workers' compensation insurance carrier. Cashing out also means you give up the right to reopen your case for "new and further disability" should your medical condition worsen within five years of the date of your injury. Options need to be carefully considered. In this chapter, I have attempted to explain the consequences of cashing out to assist you in deciding where to go.

Settlement Alternatives

1) Stipulations

A stipulation or "stips" allows you to retain your rights to lifetime medical treatment for the injured body part. You get paid your permanent disability (PD) over time at a weekly rate until it is exhausted. If you pass away before all benefits are paid out, your case is at an end and the insurance carrier is no longer obligated to pay any benefits. As noted above, if your condition worsens within five years of your injury date, you can petition the Workers' Compensation Appeals Board (WCAB) for an increase in your disability.

2) Compromise and Release

A Compromise and Release (C&R) cashes out your rights to future medical treatment and accelerates all PD in one lump sum. When you settle out your case by way of a C&R, you give up your right to future medical treatment in return for cash. As noted above, you give up your right to reopen your case. Finally, insurance companies usually insist on a full release of death benefits should an injured worker die as a result of his or her industrial injuries. Typically, other rights such at the Job Displacement Voucher benefit are also resolved in a C&R (this changes for injuries after 1/1/13—no more settlement of this benefit). The long and short of it is that the insurance carrier is released from any and all obligation to provide benefits to you after the Workers' Compensation judge approves the C&R.

3) Compromise and Release with rights to receive medical treatment

This is a rarely used, creative way of settling out disputes over permanent disability. It involves giving a person a lump sum for PD but keeping his or her medical treatment rights open.

Settlement Considerations

The safest way to settle a case is usually resolving it by stips. At least you have the right to fight for future medical treatment. Certainly, if you have no other treatment options you need to seriously consider settling this way. If you have other medical treatment alternatives, or you do not need significant treatment, a C&R is a safer bet. First of all, people need to be aware of the risks involved. Giving up your rights to receive medical treatment—when you really need it—is risky unless you have a solid alternate treatment plan.

Group/Individual Insurance

You may qualify for group medical coverage when you move to a new job or become covered by a family member's policy. Or, you may choose to get an individual policy of health coverage. The question is, will you be covered for your preexisting industrial injury?

The California Patient's Guide is a great resource for researching insurance coverage for preexisting conditions (Calpatientguide.org/v.html). As set forth in Chapter Five:

If you are joining a group health plan, you have the right to not be denied coverage on the basis of your health status, medical condition or history, genetic information, disability or insurability.

You have the right to receive coverage for preexisting conditions in most cases within 12 months (or, in some instances, 6 months) of enrolling in a health care plan.

If you are enrolling in an individual plan, you have the right not to be denied coverage if you have had 18 months of continuous coverage previously and meet certain other requirements.

You have the right to be credited for time enrolled in a previous plan against any preexisting condition waiting period.

There are simply no guarantees in life. No one can unconditionally guarantee that a group insurance carrier will pick up preexisting comp conditions—without a fight, anyway (it is called a bad faith law suit if they do not). Each case must be individually checked to see if this will work. There could always be some twists and turns that can't be foreseen. If you can treat with your group coverage or an individual policy, the down side is that you may be stuck with a deductible. The up side is that you are out from under the thumb of the workers' compensation system and controlling your own medical treatment destiny.

Public Health Benefits

Medicare

People qualify for Medicare when they have been on Social Security Disability for two years or after they have qualified for straight Social Security. Or, they become entitled to Medicare when they are 65.. Many of my clients who are on Medicare ask me if they can use their Medicare benefits instead of their medical benefits under a workers' compensation claim. My response is that Medicare takes great exception to people cashing out their rights to receive medical benefits in their workers' compensation action, spending the money on non-industrially related medical expenses, and then going on to treat with this benefit. Handled improperly, you could find yourself with no coverage through Medicare (if you cashed out your rights to medical treatment and spent the money).

There are some rather clever ways to get around the problem, some with zero risk, others like "going 90 mph in a slow zone." The first rule in settling out medical treatment rights is that Medicare will not review cases that are settled for $25,000 or less. That is their policy decision; it doesn't mean they have established a safe harbor and will not try to assert a credit down the road. It might be unlikely, but it could happen. Many people just go forward and settle out their cases on this basis with no Medicare review and take their chances. Prudent people make sure there is an allocation of part of their settlement to reasonably anticipated future medical expenses and judicially record expenditures on industrial-related medical expenses.

Other people, with larger settlements and more serious medical conditions, need to go the long route. They get the Center for Medical Services (CMS) (Medicare's administrative wing) to review an allocation of money to a "Medicare Set-Aside Account" (MSA). Thereafter, money is doled out from an account that they establish for this purpose, coupled with a yearly accounting requirement to CMS. This is, without question, the gold standard for the safest resolution of the Medicare issue.

CMS has the following review thresholds:

1) You are a Medicare beneficiary at the time of settlement and the total settlement is greater than $25,000, or

2) You are not a Medicare beneficiary at the time of settlement but there is a reasonable expectation that Medicare enrollment will occur within 30 months of the settlement, and the total settlement exceeds $250,000.

This approval process now takes up to three months (as we are dealing with the federal government here). It also involves going to a vendor and having them project the need and value of future medical treatment that is payable under the Medicare system. Then this MSA is forwarded on to CMS for their approval. Eventually, an agreement as to an appropriate set-aside amount is cut with CMS. They are happy so long as their "interests are protected." In other words, they want a sufficient amount of cash placed in an interest bearing account to be used exclusively for the industrial condition.

Medi-Cal

Some people can only qualify for Medi-Cal. Medi-Cal is an income-based benefit. In other words, if you make too much money, or have too many assets, you lose Medi-Cal entitlement. This is a huge problem for a person that has Medi-Cal as his or her only source for medical treatment. With Medi-Cal, you normally do not have go through the long acceptance process of an MSA. The problem is, if a large sum of money is laid on the table for settling out treatment rights, you lose your entitlement to Medi-Cal in the first place (and Supplemental Security Income—federal welfare—for that matter).

There is a rather clever IRS-sanctioned method for getting around this problem. It is called a Special Needs Trust. The Special

Needs Trust is a device used for people who are on income-based benefits such as Supplemental Security Income (SSI), Medi-Cal, CMS (County Medical Services), and the like. The trust is created as a device for storing money and doling it out in payments that are specifically exempt from disqualifying income and asset limitations of these programs. There are significant drafting considerations for such a trust that require the services of a seasoned professional. The general rule for trust distributions is that payments from the trust cannot be for food, clothing, or shelter. Skillful drafting of a settlement agreement, creation of Special Needs Trusts, and prudent, informed distributions can help with this big problem.

The Affordable Care Act (Obamacare), how will it affect your settlement?

The burning question my clients have been asking me lately is this: "Tom, under the ACA, can I cash out my medical rights under my workers' compensation claim and get coverage for the same medical condition with an ACA policy?" Transitioning to an ACA policy would mean coverage for the "whole person" as they like to say in comp now. It would mean no more Utilization Review denials. No more zealous defense attorneys trying to cut off pain control in cases of catastrophic injury. It would also mean dealing with a possible deductible and co-pays on medical bills.

After reviewing the ACA, it certainly appears that there are no exclusions for preexisting conditions suffered on the job. Also, there does not appear to be any provisions in the law specifically addressing subrogation or creating any right to reimbursement as between the plans. There is no indication that this new law will lead to a set-aside situation although Medicare's interests must still be considered in each case.

However, as one of my respected colleagues advised me, the truth is no one really knows how the ACA will play out. If someone was thinking about cashing out their rights to receive medical treatment in their comp actions and depend on ACA coverage, it would be smart to review the Covered California booklet first: https://www.coveredca.com/news/PDFs/CC_Health_Plans_Booklet-rev1-8-6.pdf. As they say, the devil is always in the details.

While the ACA offers low premiums for individuals and families, these affordable premiums may be moot when you consider the deductibles and co-payments that are involved with these plans. In reading the fine print, you may find that the "affordable" plan that you selected may not be so affordable. For example, under the ACA's "Silver" or midrange plans, studies in 6 states demonstrated that the average deductible for each individual is $2,550.00…that is more than double the deductible that of employer plans! A consumer reporting company also found that these new plans require patients to pay 40% on average for certain pricey prescription medications…medications used to treat many common, chronic diseases such as rheumatoid arthritis, multiple sclerosis and many others. So, choose your plan wisely…consider not only your monthly premiums, but also your coverage and your deductibles.

Reasonable Expectations

What amount of money can you reasonably expect from an insurance carrier to cash out your future treatment rights? First of all, understand that a C&R is a voluntary act on the part of both parties to the deal. If either side balks, then there is no deal. If you ask for too much, or the carrier is too cheap, everybody gets up and walks away from the table.

A judge cannot force either an insurance company or you to sign a C&R. An insurance company has less reason to settle out their responsibility to provide medical treatment if the settlement amount is equal to what they would pay over time on the claim. But medical treatment costs are astronomical, so normally there is a "sweet spot" out there that you can count on if you're reasonable.

The larger question is an insurance company's motivation to settle. It is a mystery to me sometimes. Often, an adjuster just gets stuck on an unrealistic figure and nothing happens for years. Then, they move on, someone takes over their "inventory," is given the directive to "resolve all cases," and the case gets settled.

Legacy Value of C&R/Death Consequences

As I stated above, the safest advice is to keep your medical rights intact. At least you have the right to fight for medical treatment. Even having to fight for medical treatment is better than being left out in the cold with a disabling condition and no medical coverage. That said, if someone is willing to accept some risk, there are some fairly good options out there depending on how a client is covered by public benefits, group or private insurance.

Another big issue is just having the cash. If an injured worker with stips dies, his or her claim dies too, and the insurance company gets a windfall. If you have the cash in your pocket, it goes to your estate and your loved ones. Also, there is the idea of controlling your own medical destiny as opposed to having an insurance company just saying no!

As I have said over and over, medical treatment in the workers' compensation system is "socialized medicine's evil twin." It is controlled by a pro-business, pro-insurance Labor Code that has cost savings at its core. Insurance companies make money by minimizing the claims against them. That means denying any form of medical treatment they can get away with.

While public medical benefits have their own set of unique problems, they are "entitlement based." In other words, if you qualify for them, you get the medical treatment. Individual and group insurance have their deductibles and own unique set of limitations to watch out for too.

CHAPTER SIXTEEN

WHAT DID ARNOLD AND JERRY DO TO OUR COMP SYSTEM?

"I NEVER WANT TO HURT ANY ONE OF THE WORKERS OR THE PEOPLE THAT GET THE BENEFITS"

-[*former*] *Gov. Schwarzenegger, Sacramento Bee 11/19/03*

The workers' compensation system seems to go through a huge legislative upheaval every five years or so. Most recently, Governor Jerry Brown signed SB-863 into law. Arnold Schwarzenegger signed SB-899 in 2004 and truly changed everything. To understand what you are up against, you really need to appreciate its historical context.

One Day of Infamy:

Bad things happened to working men and women in this state on April 19, 2004. That was the day SB-899 was signed into law. Unhappy with Gray Davis, Californians hired Arnold Schwarzenegger to do the job of governor. Little did they know, not only was he messing with his staff, he was messing with a system that for a hundred years had protected people injured on the job.

The first and only thing he apparently accomplished in his eight years in office was sweeping changes to the California Workers' Compensation system. He succeeded in pressuring the California legislature into passing lopsided, pro-insurance "reforms." Benefits were slashed to injured workers across the state. Billions of dollars changed hands with the stroke of a pen. Insurance companies began making money like big oil companies.

Making Sense of It All

As an advocate, it is difficult for me not to be furious about these changes. But to put these changes in their best light, what happened was what people in the securities industry call a "market correction". Premium rates paid by employers shot through the roof. Things were seriously out of balance and something had to happen.

So why did the rates shoot up? Well, years ago, people on both sides of the aisle agreed to deregulate the cost of workers' compensation policies sold to the businesses. Some carriers got really aggressive during this period of laissez-faire capitalism and sold policies below the ultimate cost of policy pay out. We were in the era of the dot-coms, and the money some of these carriers were investing their premium dollars in was less than secure.

Workers' compensation insurance companies, along with almost everyone else, lost their shorts when things went bust in the stock market crash of 2000-2002. To be brutally honest, applicant attorneys were pushing for increases in permanent disability rates in the middle of all this! What were we thinking? It was the perfect storm, as they say. So the dam started cracking in the early 2000s. Some insurance companies didn't have the money to cover operations and started going belly up. Golden Eagle, Legion, Superior National… they all stumbled and fell.

Fortunately, in California we have the California Insurance Guarantee Association (CIGA), so they started picking up claims of carriers that fell into liquidation. CIGA has a fairly narrow statutory mandate for coverage, so a huge number of claims were pushed off on the State Compensation Insurance Fund (SCIF). Medical treatment costs were skyrocketing. Something had to go. In response, the State Fund jacked up their rates astronomically. Employers were screaming. Enter Arnold.

The Fallout:

The brunt of the cost reductions fell squarely on injured workers. In the landmark report Senate Bill 899: Two Years Later, author Michael W. Sullivan pointed out that SB-899 had resulted in a 54% reduction in permanent disability paid to applicants. He also noted that the reforms had erased a $12.9 billion dollar deficit in statewide insurance company reserves, creating a $5 billion dollar surplus in its stead.

So I guess that is great news for employers, but what about the people who are actually doing the work? What happened to the "historic bargain between management and labor"? This was the very bargain that shielded employers from tort liability and in return gave injured workers compensation for their lost earning capacity, temporary disability, and medical treatment.

Some of the major changes to benefits under SB-899:

1) Temporary Disability (Payment for Lost Wages or TD)

Now, injured workers only get two years coverage for TD. If you are continuously disabled, it will most certainly end in two years—ready or not. Fortunately, most injuries take much less than two years to recover from. But what about people who have more serious injuries (think back or major joint surgery) that take longer to recover from? They are literally left out in the cold unless they qualify for other state and federal benefits.

2) Permanent Disability (Payments made for loss of earning capacity or PD)

PD is now determined by the American Medical Association's *Guides to the Evaluation of Permanent Impairment, 5th Ed.* (the Guides). The Guides are simply a mean-spirited impairment calculation protocol developed by conservative doctors who have no idea what the true cost of an industrial injury is to a working person. The Guides themselves indicate that they are not to be used to develop figures for permanent disability, but they are used across the nation because they are very stingy to workers. They aid the bottom line of big insurance companies, which is why they have been implemented cookie-cutter fashion across this country—working people here in California being the latest victims.

3) Medical treatment is now evidence-based and driven by the *American College of Occupational and Environmental Medicine Guides* ("ACOEM Guides"). The ACEOM Guides are another sad reminder of the Golden Rule-- he who has the gold, makes the rules. This protocol was, like the AMA Guides, assembled by a group of conservative industrial doctors to save money for insurance companies. SB-899 gave insurance adjusters some serious tools to limit medical treatment to injured workers, including:

a) Medical Provider Networks (MPNs). This change allows insurance companies to control (employ) the treating physicians. An injured worker no longer has free choice of who he will treat with. Now, if a doctor gets a little carried away advocating for an industrial patient, he or she gets spit out of the network like a bad seed. The days of a treating doctors going out of their way to advocate for a patient are gone forever.

b) Utilization Review (UR). UR now allows the wholesale denial of medical treatment based on the ACOEM Guides. Insurance companies needed a way to contain costs. Now, treatment has to be evidence based, which allows an insurance company to micromanage how medical treatment gets doled out. Predictably, necessary diagnostic studies such as MRIs, CAT scans, and x-rays get routinely denied based on the ACOEM Guides.

Jerry Brown and SB-863

Governor Jerry Brown signed SB-863 into law in 2012. Like SB-899, it ushered in wide-ranging changes to the compensation system. I will touch on only two here. The good news is that people injured on and after 1/1/13 are going to get a bump in their level of permanent disability on their claims. It is about time. There has been a 30% increase that has been phased in between 2013 and 2014. The bad news is the insurance industry got their way again on medical treatment issues. Medical disputes are supposedly no longer in the hands of lawyers and judges. All disputes over medical treatment will now be handled by the Department of Industrial Relations via their Independent Medical Review system (IMR). It will be HMO style decision making by doctors whom you will never see. Appellate rights are sharply limited. There are lots of unknowns here that only the next few years will clarify.

Reconciliation

It has been years since SB-899 was voted into law. It was like an atomic bomb went off in our little legal community.

But when you think about it, you have to ask yourself the question: What are we going to do about it? I have a client who suffered a very serious back injury that ultimately confined her to a wheelchair. The doctors could never understand her sunny disposition. I asked her about this once and she said, "Tom, 10% of life is what happens to you; and 90% is how you deal with it…"

So that is to be our job from here on out—dealing with it. Dusting ourselves off and fighting back. It is not an impossible task. And Arnold? Well, he is single now and back where he belongs - in Hollywood.

Made in the USA
Monee, IL
15 September 2026

63192228R00059